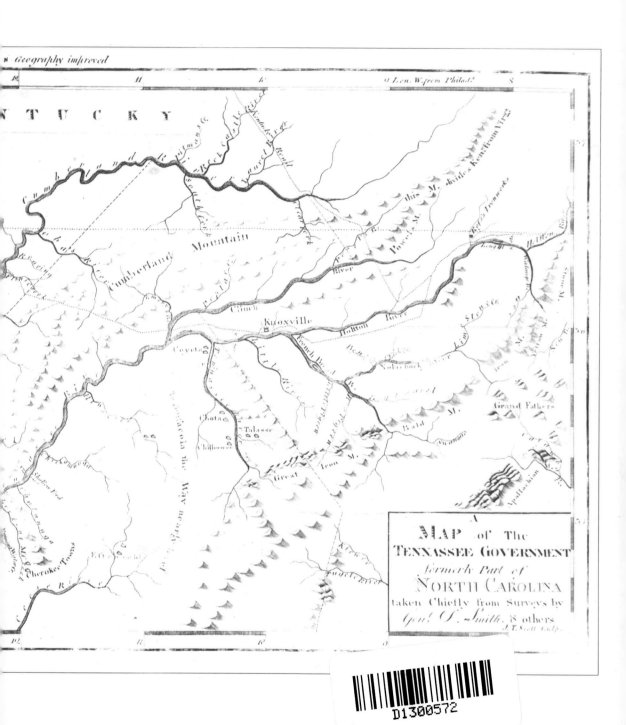

D1300572

TENNESSEE TRAILBLAZERS

TENNESSEE TRAILBLAZERS

PATRICIA & FREDRICK McKISSACK

Illustrated by Michael Sloan

MARCH MEDIA
Brentwood, Tennessee

Tennessee Trailblazers
by Patricia and Fredrick McKissack

Text copyright © 1993 by March Media, Inc.

Art copyright © 1993 by Michael Sloan

Published by March Media, Inc.
7003 Chadwick Drive, Brentwood, Tennessee 37027

Distributed by Rutledge Hill Press
513 Third Avenue South, Nashville, Tennessee 37210

All rights reserved. No part of this publication may be reproduced, stored in a retrieval system, or transmitted in any form or by any means—electronic, mechanical, photocopy, recording or any other—except for brief quotations in printed reviews, without the prior permission of the publisher.

First printing, 1993

Library of Congress Catalog Card Number: 93-77084

ISBN 0-9634824-0-8

PRINTED IN THE UNITED STATES OF AMERICA

for

Ann Elizabeth McKissack Brown
Pulaski, Tennessee

ACKNOWLEDGEMENTS

Tennessee Trailblazers celebrates the lives of Tennesseans who lived long ago, but the book itself is the work of many Tennesseans living now. It would not have come into existence without the support of the Women's National Book Association. Its members saw the need for such a book among today's young readers and continued to be interested in every part of the publishing process. Members of WNBA's special committee for this project are: Maggie Burns, Carolyn Daniel, Lila Empson, Genevieve Gebhart, Mary Glenn Hearne, Joan Medwedeff, Peg Morris, Donna Paz, Adele Schweid, Carolyn Wilson, and Nell Wiser.

Several others who have made great contributions toward publishing these stories are mentioned here:
Rutledge Hill Press for its distribution,
Nashville Area Booksellers Association for its promotional
    grant,
Steve Laughbaum who designed the words and pictures,
Alice Ewing who checked the proof of the final stories, and
Jolynn Johnson who spent many hours at the computer
    working on the text and design.

Thanks to all the above for working with the excellent words of Patricia and Fredrick McKissack and beautiful pictures from Michael Sloan. The young people of Tennessee now have stories from their state's history to enjoy for a long time.

CONTENTS

INTRODUCTION

For two centuries, a lot of outstanding people have called Tennessee "home." And their stories are as interesting and diverse as the characters who helped carve a state out of dogwood forests, pine-covered mountains, winding rivers, and fertile farmland. That's why choosing subjects for this book was so difficult.

We wanted to include individuals who represented the various ethnic groups that contributed to the state's history. We also wanted to feature people who were from different parts of the state and from different time periods. So we let a bit of timeless wisdom be our guide in deciding who to include: *You know a tree by the fruit it bears.*

Although many people were considered, we finally settled on Thomas Sharpe Spencer, Nancy Ward, Ella Sheppard (and the Fisk Jubilee Singers), and Cordell Hull. The common thread that links them all is that they were "doers." In the trailblazer's spirit they courageously accepted challenges and overcame obstacles in this land we call Tennessee.

During the time before the state was formed, the land was controlled by the Cherokee, Chickasaw, Creek, and Iroquois Tribes and explored by the Spanish, French, and English colonists. This time is presented from two points of view: Thomas "Big Foot" Spencer, a long hunter, who was the first white man to farm in the Cumberland Valley, and Nanye-hi (Nancy Ward), a Cherokee " beloved woman" who had by bravery earned a position of leadership.

Tennessee became the 16th state, admitted to the Union on June 1, 1796. For the first half of the nineteenth century, the nation debated the issue of slavery. Unfortunately the country was divided in a bloody war between 1861–1865. Tennessee, a slave state, stood with the Confederacy, but in 1866 it was the first state to be readmitted to the Union. That same year, Fisk University was started in Nashville to help educate the newly freed slaves. Ella Sheppard and several young students formed a singing group called the Fisk Jubilee Singers. They performed spirituals in concerts all over the world, earning money to build their fledgling school while preserving the music of their slave parents.

Cordell Hull served the people of Tennessee, the nation, and the world for nearly fifty years. He began as a country lawyer in middle Tennessee, but he went on to leave his mark as a judge, congressman, senator and statesman. Secretary of State Hull's leadership in forming the United Nations and his lifelong dedication to peace won him a Nobel Peace Prize in 1945.

There are many more stories yet to be told. But for now, we are proud as former Nashvillians to introduce these trailblazers to a new generation of Tennesseans.

Patricia and Fredrick McKissack

WINTER IN A SYCAMORE

THE STORY OF BIG FOOT SPENCER

Right outside Gallatin, in Sumner County, down State Highway 25, there's a stone and bronze marker at Castalian Springs. It says:

> *On this spot stood the hollow sycamore tree in which Thomas Sharpe Spencer spent the winter of 1778–79, deserted by his companions for fear of Indians. Spencer helped build at Bledsoe's Lick, 50 yards south of this spot, the first cabin in Middle Tenn., and planted the first crop of corn.*
>
> *He was killed by Indians April 1st, 1794, on the site since known as Spencer's Hill, Van Buren County, Tenn.*

This winter adventure was only one episode in the life of Thomas ("Big Foot") Spencer. He was a long hunter, an Indian fighter, and, by all reports, a man of great strength. He came from Virginia about 1776. Later he became the first

white settler to clear land, plant corn, erect a permanent dwelling, and claim title to Middle Tennessee lands.

Known as the largest and bravest man west of the Allegheny Mountains, Spencer was also reported to have feet so big that everybody called him "Big Foot" Spencer. This is his story.

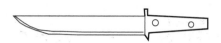

"You lost your knife?" Spencer stared at his friend John Holliday with surprised gray eyes. He growled something under his breath, then slapped his thigh and kicked at the ground with his huge left foot. Standing three heads taller than Holliday and weighing close to three hundred pounds, the angry Spencer was an awesome sight. "Are you addled, man? Or did you lose it on purpose—just to make me go back to Virginia with you?"

Holliday nervously threw a piece of driftwood on the campfire. "We done hunted on both sides of the Cumberland River and got pelts a-plenty. We done fought Cherokee, Shawnee, Chickasaw, and Creeks together. We even now planted and harvested a corn corp. I'm ready to go home." The young man swallowed hard. There was none of the usual bluster in his voice. "I got no cause to say I lost my knife just to make you come back with me."

Spencer shrugged, choosing not to speak. Fingering the sack of seed corn inside his chest, the big man remembered the first time he'd seen the green rolling hills of the Middle Cumberland. He smiled as his mind rambled back to a Kentucky campfire two years earlier and the first time he met Holliday.

Spencer had left Virginia on a hunt. A few months out he'd met five other hunters who were camping in Kentucky. Among them was John Holliday, a young, dark-eyed Virginian with a toothy smile. Ordinarily Spencer chose to hunt alone, but he'd joined their party.

They came through the Cumberland Pass in the spring and explored until fall. The area was full of wild game—all a man could hunt and eat. The soil was rich, too. Even a lazy man could mash a seed in the ground and it would grow.

After a year, the other hunters returned to Virginia. Spencer had decided to stay, clear land, plant corn, and build. Holliday had stayed with him and endured the hardships of a cold winter, spring rains, summer heat, and the joy of their first harvest. Now Holliday had no knife and a powerful hankering to go home.

Turning to his companion in earnest, the big man tried to persuade his young companion to stay. "Can't I get you to come back with me? We can winter at Bledsoe's Lick. Come Spring, we'll have first choice of the best farming land in the colonies."

The younger man considered his friend's words, then answered firmly, "No, I'll be getting on home to Virginny before Christmas. And besides," he added with a sigh, "there's a war going on. The colonies are fighting for independence. Seems right I ought to take an interest in that somehow."

"You're not a soldier. You're a long hunter."

"I know . . . but . . ."

"But what?" Spencer impatiently walked to the edge of the campfire's light. "Listen to me. You don't even have a knife! How will you manage close kills and skinning? How will you spear and clean fish? What about carving and mending?"

Holliday had a ready answer. "I've got my gun and my wits. Besides I didn't just fall through the Cumberland Gap this morning, you know."

Spencer mumbled something about not being so sure about that, when suddenly a dead tree limb crashed to the ground just outside the circle of light. The big man drew his knife in anticipation of an attack. Holliday instinctively reached for his knife, too, but it wasn't there. Poised back to back and crouched in combat positions, the two frontiersmen confronted the darkness – watching, listening, sensing the night. Nothing came. There was only the silence.

The anxious moment passed. Holliday spoke first. "A slave man once told me, if a dead tree limb falls and there's no wind blowing, expect rain."

"Superstitious nonsense!" Spencer scoffed, sheathing his knife. "Look at what's real—you standing there with bare hands. What would you've used to defend yourself if we'd been attacked?"

"The tree limb!" Holliday settled down on his elk-skin mat and pulled the patchwork of rabbit fur over his body.

But Spencer wouldn't be thrown off by the attempted humor. "You're as stubborn as . . . as . . . as . . ."

"You are," Holliday finished the sentence, making a point against which Spencer had little defense.

Moving like a man whose mind was made up, Spencer busied himself with a project only he understood. First, the big man mysteriously disappeared in the darkness, returning some moments later with a small tree branch. From it he cut a four-inch piece. After he had scraped off the bark and scored the bottom, it looked like a crude handle.

Next Spencer found a piece of buffalo hide in his pack and cut three thin strings. Methodically, he braided the strings into a measure of rope.

Holliday's dark, questioning eyes followed Spencer's movements. He leaned forward, but he didn't speak. Neither did Spencer.

Spencer's knife, an eighteen-inch blade, was longer than the ones carried by most long hunters, but suitable to his size. He placed it across the front of his knee. Taking the blade, which he'd wrapped in a skin, in one hand and the handle in the other, he pulled back with one powerful jerk and snapped the blade in two crosswise.

"Now," he said, putting one of the broken blades in the grooved-out tree limb he'd fashioned as a handle, "that rabbit is skinned." He secured the blade to the handle with rawhide strips, then handed the makeshift knife to Holliday. "You get half and I get half. Now you've got yourself a knife."

They broke camp early the next morning. Clouds hid the sun, but it was warmer than the night before. "I'll stop by and tell your folks you're alive and well," Holliday said.

There was a pause. "Don't let them cheat you over in Glasgow," Spencer mumbled.

Each man touched the other's shoulder, then they parted quickly. One turned north, the other south.

It took Spencer four full days to walk back from the border of Kentucky because he hunted along the way. He needed the fur skins to trade for supplies. He bypassed Bledsoe's Lick, where he intended to stay the winter, and

headed for French Lick, a trading post owned and operated by a Frenchman, Timothy Demonbreun.

Spencer wondered, as he approached the store, what mood Tim Demonbreun might be in that day.

"Well! It is the biggest of the big men, the Cumberland Giant himself." Demonbreun greeted Spencer with a mock salute. "I see all your companions have deserted you—even Holliday."

Spencer ignored the comment and placed his supply order quickly. He wanted to make short work of his dealings with the Frenchman. "I also need a knife." He dropped a dozen or more beaver and otter pelts on the counter. "These should take care of what I owe you."

"You owe me more, Thomas Spencer." The Frenchman pulled the furs onto his side of the counter.

Spencer looked surprised. He heard the three men sitting by the fireplace stop their conversation to watch and listen. That gave Demonbreun just the audience he needed.

Demonbreun shrugged. "What can I say? Your big feet caused one of my best hunters to run away."

"My big feet?" Spencer kept his voice calm, no sign of anger or frustration.

The Frenchman showed Spencer several knives to consider. "It seems when you were out hunting, you came upon his cabin and left your footprint in the mud. Imagine my man's horror when he came back and found the

footprint at his doorstep!" Demonbreun lapsed into French.

Then, leaning over the counter, he looked at Spencer's feet. He spread his hands about fifteen inches apart. Everybody laughed.

Meanwhile, Spencer handled the knives, tossing one in the air and catching it first with his left hand and then his right. His pleasant expression never changed.

The Frenchman hurried on with the story. "The footprint was so-o-o-o-o big, my man thought he had come into a land of giants and ran for his very life. And that man was one of my best hunters. You deprived me of income. So you owe me." The lodge shook with laughter.

Spencer leaned against the counter. He flashed a good-natured smile, then without ever changing his expression, the big man turned and with lightning speed hurled the knife. On its course, the knife whizzed past Demonbreun's ear and hit the wall behind him.

"Good balance," Spencer said matter-of-factly. "I'll take that knife."

The men around the fire were laughing again; this time not at Spencer, but at Demonbreun, whose face had turned quite pale.

After packing his supplies, Spencer tossed two rabbit furs on the counter. "These should take care of any additional debt *you say* that I owe." He turned to leave.

Demonbreun pushed the rabbit pelts to one side. "Worthless," he scoffed.

Spencer answered with a chuckle of his own. "I know."

As Spencer reached the door, one of the men by the fire, a black man who spoke with a thick French accent, called out, "I like you, beeg man. We've not met. I am DuSable, the West Indian. What's your name?"

"I am Thomas Sharpe Spencer." Then smiling over his shoulder at Demonbreun, he added, "But some folk here-about call me Big Foot."

When Spencer got back to Bledsoe's Lick the next day, a light snow had already begun to fall. The ground was cold enough for it to stick. He needed shelter for the night, but right then his need for food was greater.

Game always came to the lick, so hunting was not a big concern. The experienced hunter carefully loaded his gun from the powder horn. He hid among marsh weeds and waited as he had so many times before. In the foggy low-lands, he caught a glimpse of a rabbit darting past, followed by a fox.

But as he was trying to get a good shot off, a brown bear reared up behind him. He was at an awkward angle, so he couldn't get off a straight shot. He fell backward and his gun accidently fired. The frightened bear waddled forward,

roaring a challenge. Scrambling to his feet, Spencer spotted a hollowed-out sycamore tree with an opening shaped like an inverted keyhole. He dashed toward the tree.

A man can't outrun a bear. But Spencer was hoping the snow would slow the animal's pace just enough for him to reach the tree about thirty feet away. The bear recovered quickly and chased Spencer. Feeling the hair on his neck rise, he dived for the lower part of the opening.

The bear grunted a few more times, then dropped on all fours again. The top part of the keyhole doorway was too small for a bear to get through. The bottom, the part through which Spencer had shimmied, was another story.

The big mountain man took in his surroundings. He was inside a huge hollow tree in a room about nine feet in diameter.

Then he knew the truth. He was in the bear's den. No doubt, the bear had made the tree its winter home. Though it would be a tight squeeze, the bear could get in. It was coming in!

Spencer fell back against the wall and quickly loaded his gun. The bear had pushed the front part of its body through the opening. Spencer stayed calm, waited until the shot would be sure, then pulled the trigger.

The bear's head dropped forward limply. Spencer was safe. That night he prepared the bear skin inside the sycamore tree.

At first light, Spencer studied his situation. It was too cold and wet to build a hut, but that didn't matter. The tree would serve the same purpose. The sycamore was really a hollowed-out stump. It had decayed and dropped a soft layer of spongy wood shavings on the floor. Green lichen covered the ceiling. The room narrowed as it rose up about twenty feet. He decided to make his home there for the rest of the winter.

Spencer's daily chore was survival. Darkness comes early in winter, so every daylight hour was used to plan for the long, cold nights.

After waking one night to find a raccoon curiously rambling through his things, Spencer decided that his room was not safe enough. There was enough space overhead to make a second story. By strapping branches together, he fashioned a trapdoor. Next, he made an Indian ladder from a large tree branch with many limbs. He cut the limbs a few inches from the main trunk. When the ladder was leaned against the wall, he could climb to the trapdoor and pull the ladder up behind him. In this "secret chamber," he could keep his belongings safe and also watch the salt lick. Within days his second-story room would also serve as a hiding place.

Bledsoe's Lick was on the edge of Shawnee country. Shawnee hunting parties of seven to ten men often wandered far from their main camp on the Ohio River. During the winter it was not uncommon for small family

groups to break away from the main village and move to hunting camps.

Early one morning Spencer was startled out of his sleep by voices. The language was Shawnee. And though he couldn't speak it himself, he understood it well. Since the winter was a hard one, Spencer reasoned that the well-known salt licks in the Cumberland had drawn the Shawnee hunting party this far south. There were four, perhaps five, of them.

They went about their business of gathering salt. Meanwhile, Spencer quietly climbed the ladder to his second level. From there he could keep an eye on the hunting party. He figured it was best to stay hidden.

Even if they found the tree, the opening was deceptive. They wouldn't think a person was living inside. At least, that's what Spencer was counting on. But if, by chance, they came to investigate, the lone man on a higher level had the advantage against any attack.

Through the day Spencer watched and listened. He heard the Shawnee talking about how their leader, Blackfish, had sided with the British against the colonists in their War of Independence.

He also heard that Daniel Boone had been captured by Blackfish and adopted as a son. Five months later, Boone had escaped and made it back to Boonesborough, Kentucky, just in time to warn the settlers that the British and Shawnee would be attacking soon.

For the first time Spencer heard the name Tecumseh, another adopted son of Blackfish. The Shawnee spoke his name in a special way. Tecumseh was only fifteen, yet he already commanded that much respect. Spencer figured Tecumseh was a name he would hear again.

The hunters talked about last year's corn dance and what crops their women would plant come spring. Then, after sharing a meal of roasted rabbit, they left the lick.

After a lonely Christmas and a gloomy New Year's beginning, the weather became even worse. The days and nights seemed to melt one into the other.

Most days it would have been easier to stay snuggled in his bearskin rug. But he made himself follow a routine. He said his name, the day of the week, the date, and the year. He repeated the Twenty-third Psalm and the Lord's Prayer. Then he began the chores necessary for his survival—hunting and storing, checking his gun and powder supplies, and gathering wood. If he could do all those things, then he knew he was well and sane.

On the 26th of January, 1779, Spencer took ill. For days he had been feeling tired. Now every bone in his body ached. His head throbbed. His stomach churned. He coughed and wheezed.

Spencer touched his face; it was clammy and hot. He knew the truth, and it was horrible. "No," he whispered. "The fever!"

His chances of survival had been diminished by half. He had to break the fever before it took hold. Dressing himself took great effort, but he did it. He gathered bark from a dogwood tree and a measure of pine needles and stumbled back to his tree and collapsed.

Shivering from chills, Spencer managed to fix a tea from the dogwood bark. It was bitter but he swallowed it down. He beat pine needles into a paste and smeared it on his chest. Covering his chest with the sleeve of his flannel shirt, which had been heated by the fire, he pulled the bear skin cover up to his chin and waited to sweat it out.

Reality faded in and out. His troubled mind conjured up images, but the big man fought to keep control. The fever told him the wind sounded like his children crying or his wife calling for him to come home. But she was dead, wasn't she?

"Papa," he heard his youngest child call. Forcing himself to get up, he followed the sound. "Here," he called, stumbling into the light. "Come to me, child. Where are you?" There was no child. *The wind,* he told himself. *It was only the wind.*

"God, I promise, if I live I'll go home to see about my children," Spencer vowed.

In his delirious state, Spencer became a child again himself. He saw his brother William and his sister Mary as they had been as children. They teased him about being so much larger than all the other children. His father appeared and scolded him for allowing himself to get sick. He heard a slave woman singing a woeful song by his bedside, and he reached out to touch her.

One by one the visitors came. They were with him, yet they weren't. Whenever he tried to speak, his words choked in his throat. His lips were parched. His body shook from extremes of heat and cold.

Late in the night a terrible vision came to him. The big man knew who the dark figure was; they had met before. "No, not yet," Spencer cried out. "I'm not ready to die." His legs were weak; his body shook uncontrollably. "You will have to fight me," he cried out weakly, yet he stood to face the Grim Reaper.

"Not now; another time," the skull-faced thing whispered and vanished. Whether the encounter had been real or imagined, it was the turning point. The fever broke. Spencer had faced death and won.

Weeks passed, for the most part without incident. Spencer quickly regained his strength. Better weather came in late February and he was able to hunt again. By mid-

March it was warm enough to bathe. His beard was thick and scraggly, and his hair had grown into a thick, tangled mop. If he didn't shave soon, fleas and ticks would infest his beard and hair. He would grow it back again next fall.

A few weeks later, Spencer calculated the ground would be thawed enough to start clearing. He knew exactly where he wanted to plant and how much work it would take. But he had made a promise. First he would go back to Virginia and see about his children. And now was as good a time as any.

On his way to Virginia, Spencer stopped at Glasgow. It was there he found out that Colonel Evan Shelby had just led a two-thousand-man force from Virginia and North Carolina against the Chickamaugas because they had sided with the British.

Spencer continued on home. Good news didn't await him there. One of his brothers had been killed in the war. His children hardly knew him. The courts had taken custody of them and threatened to take them away permanently if Spencer didn't show more interest in their welfare.

Spencer went to his sister Mary and begged for help. "My dear brother," she said. "Being a long hunter and being a father is like trying to mix oil and water. Adopt the children out. Give them a chance at happiness."

"But I love my children," Spencer argued. "I provide for them better than most. No, I won't give them up."

"You show more love in giving them up than you do trying to be a father once a year. It's been two years since we've seen you, Thomas. Young Holliday brought news that you were alive. Be reasonable. I will see to it that the children are placed in fine homes."

In the end, Spencer agreed.

The British surrendered at Yorktown, Virginia, on October 19, 1781. By that time Spencer was well established as a farmer and landowner. James Robertson and John Donelson had led a group of settlers into Nashborough, downstream from French Lick. And for the next fourteen years, Thomas ("Big Foot") Spencer helped develop the Middle Cumberland. His sister Mary came to join him, and so did his brother John.

One spring in 1794, Spencer started back to Virginia to claim an inheritance. On his way back he stopped at a block house at South-West Point, near present-day Kingston. There he met Griffith Rutherford and David Wilson, both good friends of his. They introduced him to James Walker. And the four agreed to have supper together.

"So you're Big Foot Spencer," Walker said, extending his hand. Spencer was still not accustomed to handshaking, but he responded by grasping the man's hand and delivering a

fast, jerky shake. The pain in Walker's face was obvious.

"He don't know his own strength," Rutherford said, slapping Walker on the back. "You ever hear about the time. . ."

"Don't get Rutherford started on stories," said Spencer, taking a seat at a nearby table. "We'll be here all week."

Wilson ordered food for the four of them and drew up a chair. "It's best not to rile Big Foot Spencer. He don't get mad often, but when he does, look out!"

Rutherford was determined to tell his story. "See there was these two men about to fight, and Spencer come 'tween 'em to break it up. Tom Shaw, who got nothing to do with the fight, comes in and hits Spencer. Can you imagine that?"

Wilson laughed remembering the incident. He took up the story. "I remember it, too. I was there and seen it all. We held our breath, wondering what was going to come next. But Spencer here shocked us all. He picked up Shaw—who was by no means a little man—by the seat of his pants and the back of his neck and tossed him over a fence that was 'bout ten rails high."

Rutherford jumped to his feet, excitement filling his voice. "And . . . and Shaw says . . . he says, 'Mr. Spencer, if you don't mind, please pitch my horse on over the fence too, and I can be gettin' on my way.' "

Rutherford threw back his head and roared with laughter. Even Spencer had to agree it was a good story.

And that's all Rutherford needed to begin another Big Foot story. He told about the time Spencer had given Tim Demonbreun a bath in lard for slapping him with a stick. Soon they all were swapping tales about Daniel Boone and his gun "Betsy," Indians, and hunting adventures. Rutherford, Wilson, and Spencer did most of the talking. Walker listened. He was new to the territory and excited to be sitting there with such famous frontiersmen. Spencer was a little embarrassed by all the talk, and mostly just nodded modestly.

Walker looked at him in awe. "The Cherokee say you have supernatural powers."

"I'm flesh and blood, like any of you."

"Reckon we gon' get to be a state?" Figuring that Walker had heard enough stories for one day, Wilson changed the subject to politics.

"Thought we *was* a state," said Rutherford with a puzzled look on his face. "Franklin is what they call it, don't they?"

"That all fell apart in 17 'n 88. The state never got recognized," Spencer answered.

"It's true," Walker agreed. "Three years earlier John Sevier asked the U.S. to recognize Franklin as a state."

"Wasn't Greeneville the capital?" Wilson put in.

"Yep, but the whole plan failed," Spencer said softly. "'Twas my uncle, Judge Samuel Spencer, who issued the warrant to arrest John Sevier for high treason. North Carolina didn't want to give up the territory. And they still don't."

"But I've got a feeling," said Wilson confidently. "Statehood is not far off."

The hour was late. So with the promise that they would travel together through the pass, they went to bed.

The next day Spencer took the lead as usual through the pass. He knew it well. Walker asked to join him, but Wilson told him Spencer didn't ride with anybody. He'd been a solitary man all his life. But young Walker caught up with Big Foot about a mile ahead of the others.

"Back in Virginia for business or pleasure?" Walker asked, trying to start a conversation.

"Business. Settling my family estate," Spencer answered without looking at the other man.

Spencer didn't like talking while on the road. He liked to stay alert and watch for signs. He saw a spider creeping across the path. He heard a batch of chickadees fussing over their morning breakfast. What the Indians thought were Spencer's supernatural powers were actually his keen powers of observation—being aware of his world.

And his world was a beautiful place on this morning. The hills looked like they had been magically draped in white lace. The dogwoods were in full bloom.

"It is April 1, 1784," Spencer whispered to his horse. "I am well and sane."

Walker was annoyed at Spencer's total concentration on the pass ahead of them. He decided to break the silence. "I met a friend of yours some months ago. Name was John Holliday."

Spencer pulled up. "I haven't seen John in a long time. How is my old friend?"

"Just fine."

Spencer never got to say another word. They were surprised by an ambush, and a single shot killed Spencer instantly.

The others caught up quickly and fired on the ambushers. Walker, who was only slightly wounded, identified the Cherokee who shot Spencer as Double-Head, the son of Dragging Canoe, a leader among the Cherokees. Spencer's horse with saddle bags containing one thousand dollars in gold was never seen again. It was reported that the Cherokee took it, but no one really knows for sure.

☆　　☆　　☆

Tennessee became the sixteenth state two years after Spencer was buried near the trail where he fell. But no man

is ever truly dead if he is remembered. Whenever people talk about the days before Tennessee became a state, Thomas ("Big Foot") Spencer's name is bound to come up.

Spencer's tree is no longer standing. But those living in Gallatin still call the original part of their town "Spencer's choice, the site of Big Foot's homestead." No doubt children still catch catfish in Spencer's Creek. Citizens of Van Buren County named their county seat Spencer, and the place where Big Foot was killed in that same county is still remembered today as Spencer's Hill.

TWO FISH IN DIFFERENT RIVERS

THE STORY OF NANYE-HI (NANCY WARD)

The Ani-Yunwiya (the Real People) were the original hunters and caretakers of the great mountain wilderness which later became part of Tennessee. These people were called Cherokees by early white settlers, and some think the state's name comes from the name of an old Cherokee capital, Tenase.

Cherokee land was bountifully blessed with wild game, rivers and streams, and it was protected by a natural mountain barrier. When white hunters, priests, settlers, and soldiers came to the "Overhills" Cherokee country, they made contact with a proud people and negotiated a number of agreements with them. In time, all those earlier treaties would be broken and most of the Cherokee people would be driven from their homeland forever.

Nanye-hi (Nancy Ward) and her first cousin Tsi-yu Gansi-ni (Dragging Canoe) represent the two opposing views within the Cherokee Nation in the 1770s. These two leaders, who had very different approaches to dealing with the white invaders, created a tension within the Cherokee Council at a critical period. Looking back from today, we can see that their actions changed the outcome of Tennessee and American history. This is their story.

Drums and chanting at Chota announced the return of the Cherokee war party led by Oconostota, the principal war chief. Nanye-hi joined other women and children who lined the banks of the Little Tennessee River to welcome the victorious warriors. She cheered even louder when she saw her uncle, Little Carpenter, the principal peace chief. The celebration continued in the Council Hall where the war chief gave a full report of their victory.

Nanye-hi searched the Council Hall for her favorite cousin, Dragging Canoe, the son of Little Carpenter. Soon it would be time for the elders to test the children about tribal history.

Spotting him among the children of the Blue People Clan, she called him by his clan name. He didn't answer, and she knew why. Her cousin was being stubborn again—insisting that she use Dragging Canoe, the name the warriors had given him. Nanye-hi remembered how he'd gotten it.

He'd begged to go on a war party, but his father had refused. Later, in the middle of the night, Nanye-hi had helped the would-be warrior steal away in a dugout.

Just as the two of them had planned, he rowed to a hiding place where he could intercept the war party on their way to battle. "They will have to let me go with them," he'd said. "There won't be time for them to bring me back."

The plan went smoothly up to that point. He had surprised his father, Little Carpenter, at a point downstream. The boy was allowed to tag along. Then they reached a sandbar in the water. The older, experienced warriors easily dragged their canoes across the sand and continued on their way.

"If you plan to come with us, you must drag your own canoe," said Little Carpenter.

The boy stubbornly grabbed one end of the canoe and tried to pull it through the sand. The war party rowed away. But as they left the little warrior behind struggling with his beached canoe, the men cheered his bold determination. "Tsi-yu. Gansi-ni! Dragging Canoe!"

He came back to Chota hurt and humiliated. But a few weeks later, the war party returned under the red flag of victory. And when the clan heads had given their report of what had happened, several of the men told about a brave young warrior from the Wolf Clan, who would join them one day soon. "As a warrior he will be known as Tsi-yu. Gansi-ni—Dragging Canoe!"

And now he wouldn't answer to any other name. "Dragging Canoe! Over here," Nanye-hi called. Hearing that name, the boy turned and waved to his cousin. Nanye-hi hurried over to sit beside him. The questioning was about to begin.

"Why does our Council Hall have seven sides?" Little Carpenter asked the first question.

Nanye-hi answered before the other children. "So that all seven clans of our people are represented: We are the Wolf Clan. Then there are the Deer People, the Bird People, the Paint People, the Wild Potato, the Long Hair, and the Blue People."

Nods of praise passed among the headmen. She spoke well to be so young. She thought there was a smile on her uncle's face, even though he was not supposed to show favor among the children.

Dragging Canoe stood and was recognized. Like his father, the boy had a tall body and straight back. And both father and son looked at the world through strong, dark, eyes. The boy began: "Seven is also our special number. There are seven heavens, seven directions, seven clans, seven great ceremonies, and seven sacred trees."

He, too, had used words well. Oratory was believed a special gift of the Great Spirit, given to the few who were to be leaders. Little Carpenter could not conceal his pride. In fact, he didn't even try.

"Who was the first Cherokee man?" a headman of the Long Hair Clan asked.

"Kanati," the children answered together.

"Who was the first woman?"

"Selu!" they chanted in unison.

"And who gave the Cherokee corn?"

"The great spirit Agawela."

The questioning went on for another ten or fifteen minutes. At the end, Oconostota nodded his approval to Little Carpenter. "The children of Chota have been well taught. You have made us proud. We are pleased."

Later that night after all the official ceremonies were over, Little Carpenter spent time with his family. There in the quiet of his home, he didn't have to be a leader. He could just be uncle, brother, father, and husband.

Nanye-hi longed to hear one of her uncle's stories, but her mother Tame Doe had warned her not to be worrisome. Nanye-hi was happy when one of the younger children, seeing his uncle light his pipe, asked, "Will you tell us how we got tobacco?"

Little Carpenter puffed on his pipe. Circles of smoke climbed around his head. "Long ago, the Cherokee had no tobacco. Once one of our warriors was taken captive by a people far away. It was among these people that our ancestor learned about tobacco. The warrior fell in love with a maiden who taught him how to change his body shape. So to escape he changed into an hummingbird. Before flying away he tried to steal some tobacco leaves, but he was too small. Instead he took some of the seeds and brought them back to us. From that time on, we Cherokee have grown our own tobacco."

That was one of Nanye-hi's favorite stories, but she wanted to hear about her uncle's trip across the Great Sea. "Will you travel on the Great Sea again?"

It was all the encouragement her uncle needed. He was always ready to tell about his year-long adventure in England from 1730 to 1731.

"I came home a new man with a new warrior name, Little Carpenter. It was given to me by my English friends because I could build a good peace treaty from many different parts. I was the youngest of the seven Cherokee warriors who went on a peace-seeking mission to London." The children had heard the story many times, but they never tired of hearing it.

After some questions were asked about England and how far away it might be, Little Carpenter continued. "Not one of our people would go. Mr. Wiggam, the interpreter, pressed me to accept his invitation. He assured me that the distance was very much magnified and that I should be back by the end of summer or at least sometime in the fall, upon which assurance I agreed to go . . . ."

The younger children soon fell asleep, but Nanye-hi and Dragging Canoe hung on every word. He thrilled them with tales about the big man-of-war ship, the *Fox*, which had sped them across the Big Water.

Nanye-hi closed her eyes and tried to imagine what King George's court must have looked like to her uncle. But the part she liked best was the formal signing of the pledge of friendship between the two nations—England and Cherokee.

"I would love to go there and see it for myself," Nanye-hi whispered to her cousin. "Wouldn't you?"

"Not really," Dragging Canoe responded boldly.

"Why? Don't you like the whites?" his little cousin questioned.

"That's not it. There are parts of the Cherokee Nation that I haven't seen. When I have seen my own, then maybe I'll be interested in seeing what the white men have to show me."

For ten years, each October ushered in another new year for the Cherokees. Dragging Canoe became a great hunter, warrior, and chief among his people. He made a name for himself as an eloquent speaker and honored his father and the Wolf Clan whenever he spoke at the High Council. Everybody knew it was only a matter of time before Dragging Canoe would become a national leader.

And in those ten years Nanye-hi had grown into a strong and courageous young woman. Many young men had asked for her hand in marriage, but she gave her pledge to King Fisher. Nanye-hi made plans for the big day.

First, Tame Doe helped Nanye-hi build the couple's dwelling and make the necessary sacrifices that would insure peace and happiness. Then fruits and meat were dried and a packet of seed corn stored for planting in the spring.

On the morning of the wedding, the older married women visited, bringing bits of Cherokee wisdom: "A person who always complains is never pitied" or "If you hold a hot frying pan, don't blame it if you burn yourself." Nanye-hi thanked each one for coming.

At midday Nanye-hi washed her hair in a mixture made from the red hull of sumac berries. It made her hair shine. Then girlfriends and sisters fussed over the bride, braiding her hair with colorful strips of ribbon. Using clam shell tweezers, Nanye-hi arched her eyebrows and shaped them artistically.

The bride met the groom under a large sycamore tree. There the couple exchanged the traditional marriage gifts. "For you, my husband," Nanye-hi said, giving King Fisher an ear of corn. It symbolized that she intended to be a good wife.

"For you, Tisistuna-gis-ke, my wild rose," he said, handing her a leg of venison. It was his way of promising that he would always bring food for the family. With that, according to Cherokee custom, they were married.

"Welcome to the Wolf Clan," said Tame Doe, Nanye-hi's mother. And when two children, Catherine and Little Fellow, were born, Tame Doe was there to welcome them into the Wolf Clan too.

The years passed quickly and happily. But in the spring of 1755, the war drums were beating again. The Cherokee army was mobilizing.

War chiefs from the upper and middle towns had been arriving in Chota for the past two weeks. Hundreds of warriors from the valley towns in western North Carolina were massing on the Nottely and Valley rivers, waiting for Oconostota to give the word. Nanye-hi knew that her favorite cousin would be among the fighting men who would come to debate war.

Oconostota spoke before the council. "The Creeks must be driven off our land. They have attacked our lower settlements and invaded our towns along the Tugaloo River. It must stop."

The Cherokee declared war on the Creeks, and Nanye-hi followed her husband into battle. Five hundred warriors clashed at Taliwa.

Crouched behind a log, Nanye-hi helped by chewing her husband's bullets. Chewed bullets would tear the flesh of their enemies.

Suddenly, King Fisher fell, fatally wounded. Fear and grief tore at the young woman's heart. Her husband was dead! But steeling her nerve, she fought back tears—time to cry later.

I can shoot a gun, she thought. And she was a good marksman too. So she picked up her dead husband's gun, loaded, and fired. A Creek warrior fell . . . and another . . . and another. Nanye-hi held her ground throughout the battle, which raged for hours. Seeing her courage gave the outnumbered Cherokee warriors the heart to keep fighting. In the end they won.

Later, back at Chota, Oconostota told the council that Nanye-hi had been the person around whom the warriors had rallied. Her bravery had given them courage to defeat the Creeks and drive them away from Cherokee land once and for all.

For her show of bravery in battle, Nanye-hi was named a Ghighau. "You are the Beloved Woman," said Little Carpenter, giving her a swan's wing as the symbol of her authority. "The Great Spirit will speak through you. All power is yours. Use it wisely and for the good of your people."

Although she was still a young woman, she would now be head of the Woman's Council. These women held the tribe's welfare as their main concern.

At a very special ceremony, Little Carpenter escorted Nanye-hi to her seat next to him and Oconostota in the Holy Area, near the ceremonial fire.

☆   ☆   ☆

Meanwhile, Dragging Canoe had also become a strong leader among his people. With the Creeks defeated, Dragging Canoe turned his attention to whites who were coming into Cherokee lands.

"The Creeks are no longer a concern," he said. "We were outnumbered, but our superior strength and ability gave us the victory. While we are strong, we need to turn our attention to the whites who continue to come into our land."

"The English have been among us for many years," said Little Carpenter. "They are at peace with us and we with them. What is the problem?"

Dragging Canoe leaped to his feet. "The whites are no big problem now. But more and more of them are coming. Even now they are building a fort in the shadow of our capital. I say we stop them now, while we can, or we *will* have a problem."

"If a man spends all his time looking for snakes under logs, he will starve to death." The Beloved Woman used one of the many wise sayings that she often used to make a point.

Dragging Canoe's eyes flashed anger. He pulled himself erect and answered with another proverb: "A person who looks may not see." He left the Council Hall. Later, he moved to a town in the Valley region. There he became a strong war chief and led one of the attacks against Fort Loudon. Dragging Canoe sought every opportunity to drive whites from the Cherokee lands.

Meanwhile, Nancy allied herself with Little Carpenter who encouraged peaceful solutions between white and Cherokee.

☆   ☆   ☆

The first time Nanye-hi saw Brian Ward, he had been captured by Dragging Canoe and a party of warriors. They had brought him to Chota to stand trial as a spy. Ward protested that he was just an English trader, traveling through the Overhills country in search of game. Although Little Carpenter tried to help, Ward was Dragging Canoe's prisoner and under his jurisdiction. It was his right to pass sentence.

"The gauntlet!" Dragging Canoe proclaimed.

That meant certain death for Ward. Two rows of warriors lined up, facing each other. Then the victim was forced to run down the corridor while war clubs and spears slashed at him from behind. There wasn't much hope for Ward.

But just as they were about to carry out the sentence, the Beloved Woman appeared. The swan's wing, symbol of her position, rested on her forearm.

"Stop," she demanded. Dragging Canoe's glance was chilling, but even he dared not challenge the Beloved Woman. "There might be more sport in a foot race," she said.

Dragging Canoe looked surprised. "Yes," he agreed quickly. "The distance of twenty miles." Nanye-hi could tell he liked the idea. "If Ward is caught, he'll be scalped and the winner will be greatly honored. If he wins, he will go free."

Good! Dragging Canoe had set the rules. And that was exactly what Nanye-hi wanted her cousin to do.

The race was set for three days later, barely enough time for Little Carpenter and Nanye-hi to prepare Ward for the run for his life.

"What is your name?" Ward asked. "Why are you trying to help me?"

"I don't believe in killing without good reason," she answered honestly. "I am Nanye-hi."

"Nancy."

"No, Nanye-hi."

"I understand, Nancy," and he smiled warmly. The woman returned his smile. There was something good and honest about Brian Ward. She liked him.

While coaching him about the race, she shared stories about her people and their customs. He told her about his life and travels in Virginia and North Carolina.

The night before the race, Nancy gave Ward a drink made with honey, herbs, and roots. "It will give you energy," she promised. "And you will need it."

When the sun rose on the third day, the race began. Ward was given a fifteen-minute lead.

Nancy didn't tell Ward, but she planned to use her pardoning power. She knew he would be overtaken very quickly, but the Cherokees respected bravery and courage. If Ward put up a good showing, then the runners would be more willing to accept Nancy's pardon with less grumbling.

Meanwhile, Little Carpenter and Nancy went into Chota to be at the finish line to serve as judges. Couriers from the fifteen-mile marker had already announced that Ward was still on his feet, but three Cherokees were only a few yards behind him.

Ward had done much better than Nancy had expected. From a hillside, she viewed the last few miles. All the other runners had dropped out except two—Dragging Canoe and one other.

Ward was hardly able to stay on his feet. He looked over his shoulder. The finish line was a few yards away. Nancy's plan had worked better than she'd hoped. The people cheered in admiration for the white foreigner who had outrun some of their best runners.

But Dragging Canoe was gaining. Ward looked back again. It was a costly look. He stumbled, losing valuable ground.

Suddenly, Dragging Canoe dived forward and tackled Ward from behind. The two men fell only a few feet from the finish line.

The warrior pulled his knife and was about to kill Ward, but the Beloved Woman stepped out of the crowd. The people parted to let her come forward.

"No!" she shouted. "Who among you will say this man should die a coward's death?"

She searched each person's eyes. Then stooping, she pulled Ward's body across the line. Dragging Canoe was furious, but he had no choice but to bow to the ruling of his cousin.

Later Nancy tried to speak to her cousin in private, but he was still angry with her. "We are two fish swimming in different rivers, Nanye-hi. We no longer speak the same language."

"Your way will only bring hatred and death to our people," she said. "In war there are no winners." But he had disappeared into the darkness.

Ward stayed in Chota and soon he and his "Nancy" were married. Up until that time she had been called by her Cherokee name, Nanye-hi. But after she married Ward, she officially changed her name to Nancy Ward. They had a daughter, Elizabeth.

☆　　☆　　☆

Over the years, Nancy became more convinced that Cherokees would benefit from peaceful contact with whites. Dragging Canoe disagreed with her passionately. Often the cousins clashed in council meeting.

Nancy's most effective argument against Dragging Canoe's position was the years of peaceful living the Cherokee had enjoyed under Little Carpenter's leadership. But Dragging Canoe countered that more and more settlers were living on Cherokee lands. "They build houses and plant crops," he said. "They plan to stay."

Little Carpenter and Nancy encouraged the first of the Overmountain settlements at Watauga, headed by James Robertson. Carter's Valley followed, led by John Carter. Evan Shelby helped to settle Holston, and Jacob Brown formed the community of Nolichucky. Nancy welcomed the settlers and helped them whenever she could.

In May 1772, the Watauga settlement sent James Robertson and John Bean to visit Chota. They made contact with Nancy Ward and told her their plans. With her help

Robertson and Bean successfully negotiated a ten-year lease from the Cherokee for Watauga lands.

The success of the Watauga deal encouraged other land speculators such as Richard Henderson from England. He approached the council about buying a large tract of land for the Transylvania Company.

A big council meeting was called to discuss the proposed land sale. Dragging Canoe came to Chota, and for the first time in many years he visited his cousin's lodge. They sat by the fire and talked the way they had as children.

"I have come to ask your help," he said.

Nancy realized it had taken a great deal for her cousin to ask for help. "I will do what is possible."

"This land sale is a bad thing. If we let our land be taken in this way, we will give up who we are."

"Little Carpenter plans to sign— "

Dragging Canoe interrupted with a raised hand. "My father would give away his arm in the name of peace. But that is not real peace. What is wrong with fighting the bear that attacks my lodge?"

"What is so different about the whites?" she argued. "They marry, have children, build houses, grow crops, hunt and fish, get sick . . . grow old and die, the same as we do."

"No, they are different. As long as we are giving, the whites take. When the Cherokee decide to take, then we are called heathens."

"It is a matter of understanding. Living together will help lessen these problems. Besides we need the trading goods they have offered for our struggles against the Chickasaws."

Dragging Canoe sighed. "I knew you would not stand with me against the whites. But you must understand that there can be no peace as long as whites live on Cherokee land. As we defeated the Creeks, so it will be with the whites!"

"You must do what you think is right, Dragging Canoe. And so must I."

The next day Nancy came to the meeting with Little Carpenter. Just as he had promised, Dragging Canoe argued forcefully against the land sale, but he was out-numbered. Little Carpenter and the council voted to sell the land. Rather than be a part of it, Dragging Canoe left before the signing.

"We are not yet conquered!" he shouted. "We will make a dark and bloody ground."

Nancy stood beside her uncle when he made his mark on the treaty, March 17, 1775, at Sycamore Shoals. He and the council signed over 20 million acres between the Kentucky River and the Cumberland River for 2,000 pounds sterling and goods worth 8,000 pounds.

A year later, the Declaration of Independence was signed by the thirteen colonies, declaring themselves independent of English rule. While the whites were fighting each other, Dragging Canoe declared war on both sides.

It was mid-August, time for the green corn dance. Members from the seven clans had been arriving in Chota all week, and preparations for the ceremony were almost complete.

Drums announced the coming of Dragging Canoe and his party. Nancy came out to greet him. Although he spoke courteously his words were formal and cold. There was anger in his dark eyes. Nancy followed her cousin to Little Carpenter's lodge. Even with his father, Dragging Canoe remained hard-faced. The years had strained their relationship to the breaking point.

"The whites are fighting each other," Dragging Canoe said. "This is the time to strike while they are divided."

"It is in our best interest to stay out of the white man's struggle," Little Carpenter answered.

Rather than be disrespectful, Dragging Canoe didn't argue. He left as soon as it was polite to leave.

"My son is a strong leader," Little Carpenter told Nancy. "Many of our people agree with him. I fear he will lead us into war very soon. You must do whatever you can to stop him,"

Nancy promised that she would, but she knew it wasn't going to be easy. That evening Dragging Canoe and his men seized four white traders who were working in Chota.

"They are spies," Dragging Canoe told the council. "We must attack the settlements before they attack us!"

Nancy was surprised at how much support Dragging Canoe had. She stepped in, trying to change the attention of the meeting. "We should not forget why we are here," she said. "This is the corn feast, a time to celebrate the blessing of corn. Let us smoke the ritual pipe of purification to cleanse our minds and hearts so the Cherokee will stay strong."

"No," said Dragging Canoe, challenging his cousin. He held a pipe up for all to see. Nancy recognized it right away. "Let us smoke the war pipe together and attack the settlements and drive out our enemies!"

The clan leaders quickly agreed and soon the war pipe was passed from one to the other. Nancy had failed to stop Dragging Canoe.

As part of the ceremonies, she carried out the tradition of making a "black drink" for the braves before battle. Stepping forward, she began the ritual around the fire.

The white swan's wing in her hand swept back and forth. Nancy chanted the words from long ago as she mixed leaves for the scalding drink. But her heart was heavy and she was glad when the ceremony was over.

Dragging Canoe stopped her as she left the Council House. He was painted for war. "Now is the time to drive the whites off our land," he said proudly. "We must take back what is ours."

"At the cost of how many of our people?" Nancy asked. "We can build a peace as Little Carpenter did in the past. The same sky covers us all."

Dragging Canoe sneered and turned his back. But he did not speak to her again.

Nancy was more troubled than ever. As she walked out into the night, she knew what she must do. She went quickly to the stockade and released the four white prisoners.

She gave them an urgent message for the Overhill settlers, warning them about Dragging Canoe's plans. "You must tell your people they are in danger. They will be attacked within two weeks. Gather your women and children into the forts for protection."

When the Indian forces attacked, white sharpshooters were ready. Even Dragging Canoe himself was wounded. The Indian warriors had to retreat and the settlements were saved.

Nancy did not believe that war was the way the Cherokee should take. Without her timely warning, most of the settlers at Watauga, Holston, and Carter's Valley would have been surprised by the Indians and killed. Without these settlements there would not have been an Overmountain men's army to defeat the English General Ferguson at King's Mountain. Without that victory the story of America could have been very different.

Little Carpenter, who favored the British, kept the Cherokee out of the conflict between the white brothers. Nancy sided with the colonists who wanted to be independent from Great Britain. Meanwhile, Dragging Canoe, encouraged by the British officers, planned attacks against the Overhill settlements. The Cherokee nation was becoming as divided as the rest of the country.

At harvest time of that same year, 1776, a delegation of fourteen chiefs came to Chota and tipped the scales against the colonists. These chiefs represented the Iroquois, Mohawks, Delaware, Ottawas, Nantucas, Shawnee, and Mingo. The chiefs had come to form a federation of all eastern tribes to stop the takeover of their lands. They made Dragging Canoe their leader.

"We are not yet conquered!" was his rallying call. Dragging Canoe had recovered from his wound. He vowed to fight until the Cherokee had regained their lands, and plans were made to attack the settlements.

For sixteen years, Dragging Canoe continued to strike at the settlements from his stronghold in the mountains. He became the principal Cherokee-Chickamauga war chief. He refused to sign any treaties or to barter away any land claimed by his people. But in the end he was defeated. He died in 1792, following a war dance ceremony at Lookout Mountain.

Nancy Ward lived on until 1822, moving from place to place as the fortunes of the Cherokee changed. One of her great-grandsons was only four years old when she died, but he tells of seeing a light rise from her body, leave through an open door, and move away toward Chota, the capital of the Cherokee nation.

Nancy was buried in Polk County near Benton, Tennessee. In the fall of 1923, her grave was marked with a bronze and stone tablet. It reads as follows:

In Memory of
Nancy Ward
Princess and Prophetess
of the Cherokee Nation
The Pocahontas of Tennessee
The Constant Friend
of the American Pioneer
Born 1738–Died 1822

SINGING IN TROUBLED TIMES

THE STORY OF ELLA SHEPPARD,
PIANIST FOR THE FISK JUBILEE SINGERS

Fisk University in Nashville, Tennessee, was founded shortly after the Civil War. It is the oldest African American college in the state and second oldest in the country. But in 1870, the school's future looked bleak. How Fisk was saved is one of Tennessee's most treasured stories.

Ella Sheppard was one of Fisk's first students and an original member of the Fisk Jubilee Singers. She, like most of the other singers, had been a slave with little or no formal musical training. But when she came to Fisk, her musical ability impressed George White, the school treasurer and music teacher. With Ella as the group's pianist, he organized the Fisk Singers and set out on a bold fund-raising venture.

The music they shared with the world helped save their school and preserve the songs of African American slaves. Most important of all, Ella and the group set a high standard of excellence and achievement. That was the beginning of the Fisk Jubilee Singers.

Ella looked at the burned-out school building. The tears pressed against the back of her eyes. *No, I will cry later,* she decided. Although only ten of her thirty-five students had come to school, they needed her to be strong.

"Come, children," she said, trying to sound older than her sixteen years. "We will have class under that big oak."

"Miz Sheppard, Miz Sheppard," one of her students called. "Who burn our school?"

"My daddy say the Ku Klux Klan set it on fire," one of the older boys put in. "They don't want us coloreds to have school here in Gallatin. Ain't it so, Miz Sheppard?"

"Isn't it so," Ella gently corrected the boy's grammar. Then taking the hands of two of the younger children, she led her class to the shade of the tree. That would be their classroom for the day.

The questions continued. "Annie's mama didn't let her come this morning. She said the Klan was gon' get us all. Is the Klan gon' get us, Miz Sheppard?"

Ella had heard plenty about the Ku Klux Klan since arriving in Gallatin from Cincinnati. She knew some people in these parts agreed with General Nathan Bedford Forrest who had started the Klan down in Pulaski. Even though the Civil War had ended five years ago, these men still refused to accept the basic rights of newly freed slaves.

"Miz Sheppard, do you think the Klan gon' come get us?"

Ella pulled herself tall. The Klan could do terrible things to people, but she didn't want to scare the children. "We have come too far to be turned around by a bunch of mean-spirited people. Besides," she said winking her eye, "didn't my Lord deliver Daniel?"

In her clear soprano voice, Ella began the old spiritual she'd heard her father sing in troubled times.

Didn't my Lord deliver Daniel,
Deliver Daniel, deliver Daniel?
Didn't my Lord deliver Daniel,
And why not every man?

He delivered Daniel from the lion's den,
Jonah from the belly of the whale.

And the Hebrew children from the fiery furnace,
And why not every man?

At the end of the verse, the children were clapping and ready to join in singing the chorus.

Didn't my Lord deliver Daniel,
Deliver Daniel, deliver Daniel?
Didn't my Lord deliver Daniel,
And why not every man?

When the song ended, Ella applauded and praised them. She felt more confident; they all did. Singing had always made her feel better. "Try not to worry," she said. "We're going to have school today, tomorrow, and as long as you keep coming."

"But how we gon' have school with no books and such, Miz Sheppard?"

"We will make a way!"

Ella found a bare spot on the ground and smoothed it out with her foot. Then searching around, she found a sharp stick. Kneeling in the dirt she wrote: F R E E D O M.

"Who knows this word?"

Hands waved for recognition. Ella singled out Abe, one of the older boys. He was twelve, perhaps thirteen, but like so many of her students, he'd never been to school before. They all wanted to learn so badly, but none more than Abe.

"That word is *freedom*," he said proudly.

You're right. Now do you know what it means?"

Abe smiled broadly. "Yes, ma'am. We're free. No more slaves. Never again can one man own another in this country!"

"Good enough," she said, smiling. "And that means you have rights. You have a right to an education. And no sheet-wearing bullies can stop you! Any of you—us. Do you understand?"

"Yes ma'am," the children chorused.

Abe's answer touched Ella's own spirit. She couldn't remember being owned. Her father had bought her freedom when she was just a baby. Then he had taken the family to Ohio. Most of Ella's students had been freed by the Emancipation Proclamation. Freedom had a completely different meaning for them. *No more slavery!*

Ella taught the rest of the term. Then, with the six dollars she'd saved, she enrolled in Fisk School in Nashville. There she planned to get advanced training in education.

Nashville in 1868 was the scene of many political clashes. All across Tennessee, equal rights and justice were under attack. Northern radicals were criticized for helping blacks build schools and businesses and for supporting black voting rights. Most of the native whites wanted to keep the South the way it had always been—insisting that people of color should "stay in the same place in freedom as they did in slavery." There were a lot of people like Ella who just wanted a fair chance to do something with their lives.

Ella had received a letter from President Ogden at Fisk. It told her to report to Mr. George White, the school's music teacher, when she arrived on campus. "He is very curious about your musical abilities," he wrote.

The old Union army barracks that housed Fisk School weren't nearly as grand as Ella had imagined. After being greeted by the female principal and finding her room, she hurried over to Mr. White's classroom. Several students were already there.

As was the custom, Mr. White and two other young men stood when Ella entered the classroom. She curtsied to them and took the seat next to a girl who spoke warmly. "Hello. I'm Jennie Jackson."

Ella liked the way the girl spoke, and she made up her mind instantly that she and Jennie would be friends.

One of the young men stepped forward. "I'm Isaac Dickerson and this is Benjamin Holmes." He turned to the other.

"I am George White. Thank you for coming," Mr. White said in a quiet, confident manner. "You all have your studies to do, and many of you have jobs after class. But I'd like to produce the cantata *Esther* this year. And I hope you will help me—especially you, Ella. I hear you have had formal music training."

"Yes, sir, I had piano lessons beginning when I was about twelve. My teacher said I had a good ear for music." Ella decided not to tell him how she had been made to go in the back door of her teacher's house. A lot of people in Cincinnati thought a black child couldn't—or shouldn't—be taught music. But Mr. White seemed glad to have someone with her talents.

"I've never had formal training," he said. "But I've always loved music. I'd be proud for you to be our pianist."

Ella tried not to shout for joy. "I'd be honored to help," she answered.

Ella almost skipped as she and Jennie walked back to their quarters. "I love this place," she said.

"Wait 'til it rains," Jennie whispered, with a chuckle and a mischievous twinkle in her eyes.

A few days later, Ella understood what Jennie had meant. It began to rain and the roof leaked like a waterfall. The old army barracks were falling down around them piece by piece. Still there was an infectious spirit that ran through the faculty and students. Besides, Ella wasn't a quitter. She grabbed a bundle of rags and, on her hands and knees, started mopping up the water. She sang while she worked—a song she remembered from her childhood.

Keep a inchin' along;
Keep a inchin' along;
Jesus will come by-an'-by.
Keep a inchin' along like a poor inchworm.
Jesus will come by-an'-by.

Others joined her, adding harmony.

Keep a inchin' along;
Keep a inchin' along;
Jesus will come by-an'-by.
Trials and trouble are on the way.
Jesus will come by-an'-by.
But we must watch and always pray.
Jesus will come by-an'-by.

When they'd finished singing, the work was finished too. That's when Ella noticed Mr. White had been standing in the doorway listening to them sing. He smiled before moving on.

Within the week, he had assigned the parts for *Esther*. Isaac Dickerson sang the part of Haman, and Ella played Esther. Rehearsals inched along like the song, note by note.

The cast practiced for months, mostly voice drills, led by Ella. *Ah-eh-ee-o-oo*—over and over in every key, until Mr. White was satisfied with the quality of the sound. And satisfying Mr. White was not easy. He pushed and pushed, striving for excellence.

Finally in the early spring of 1870, they were ready. On opening night the group performed to a packed house, and Mr. White was the first to express his joyous congratulations. Later, at a reception held in the home of a Fisk patron, Mr. White told his singers, "You were outstanding! I am proud to be associated with each one of you."

"Thanks for believing in us," Isaac said, shaking Mr. White's hand and presenting him with a gift from the cast. "It's just a small token of our appreciation. We hope you like it."

One look at Mr. White left no doubt in anybody's mind that he was proud of his students. "This is just the beginning," he said.

And sure enough, he took the Fisk choir to Memphis to perform at the opera house and later that spring to Chattanooga. Both tours were successful.

During the summer of 1870, Ella and Isaac taught school in rural areas. Ben went back to his tailor's shop. Jennie stayed in Nashville and did laundry for the Whites. But all the music students returned from their summer jobs.

Whenever President and Mrs. Ogden had a dinner party at Fisk, they usually asked a music student to provide the entertainment. One February evening, Ella was invited to play the piano.

"You look lovely," Jennie said, tying the bow on the back of Ella's dress.

"Yes," Ella said, laughing. "But I've got on your cape, Jennie, and lace gloves from Alice, and Anna's broach, and Lucy's purse.

Now all the girls were laughing. "Who will know?" Anna asked.

"This way, we'll all be there with you when you play for the president and his company," Alice added.

"Maybe one of his guests will see how talented you are and give a sizeable donation to the school," Jennie said.

Ella adjusted her skirt. "The school sure needs the money," she said. "Rumor has it that we don't have enough to last—"

"Don't say it," Jennie interrupted. "Rumor is not a dependable source. Now go and do us all proud."

After all the guests had arrived, Mrs. Ogden graciously seated them. Ella played the piano softly while the dinner was served. Several times Mrs. Ogden nodded her approval of the pieces she had selected to play.

Ella couldn't help but overhear the table conversation. President Ogden congratulated Governor W.C. Brownlow for declaring martial law in nine counties to stop Klan violence.

"As I see it, you really had no choice," President Ogden said. "They were determined to take the law into their own hands."

Good. The Klan needed to be stopped, Ella thought, remembering how they had burned her school.

A tall, dark-eyed man with a tangle of greying hair sat next to President Ogden. "The KKK would undo everything we have accomplished," he said, forcefully. "I think belonging to that organization should be against the law."

"The Klan Act is before Congress now, General," said Mrs. Ogden.

So this was General Samuel O. Armstrong. Ella had read in the paper that he was coming to Nashville. He was a commanding figure. He had been a Union officer in charge of black soldiers. After the war he'd stayed on in Virginia. Investing a large amount of his own income and borrowing the rest, he'd bought an old plantation and started the Hampton Normal and Agricultural Institute in 1868. He had come to Nashville to lecture at the convention of the National Teachers' Association of the United States.

"I'm looking forward to your speech," President Ogden said to General Armstrong. "Our choir has been invited to perform at the convention."

"In fact, the pianist for the group is Ella Sheppard," Mrs. Ogden said proudly. "She's playing for us tonight."

During the course of the meal, the conversation shifted from the Klan, to the Thirteenth, Fourteenth, and Fifteenth Amendments. Mrs. Ogden thought it was shameful that a voting rights amendment was ratified without including women. "It will just call for another amendment at a later date," she said.

The men were silent. Governor Brownlow changed the subject. "Tell me," he said to General Armstrong. "Hampton is two years younger than Fisk, yet Hampton seems to be growing at a rapid rate. How do you account for its success?"

Ella's ears perked up when she heard President Ogden add, "I've been thinking about making some changes in our program here."

Suddenly the General's eyes sparkled with excitement. Talking about his school obviously made him happy. "First, you need a fine faculty."

A bit of school rivalry stiffened Ella's back. *We have a great faculty*, she wanted to say, but kept still.

General Armstrong was beaming. "The best way to educate the large number of newly freed slaves," he continued, "is in the manual skills and crafts. At Hampton we stress self-discipline, honesty, morality, thrift, dignity, and cleanliness. We turn out bricklayers, carpenters, tailors—all fine craftsmen. Our graduates are 'doers'."

Humph! thought Ella, *I'd rather be a thinker!* Her fingers stumbled over the keys. She accidently hit a loud D-flat chord, a very sour note.

She felt better when President Ogden responded. "I can't argue with you about Hampton's being a fine school," he said. "But our program here at Fisk is excellent, too."

Mrs. Ogden pulled herself straight. "We stress art, music, literature, science, and math. We encourage our graduates to reach for the stars."

Ella wanted to applaud, but she kept playing. General Armstrong looked shocked. "But that isn't practical, madam."

"No, it isn't," retorted Mrs. Ogden. "But we're doing fine."

After the dinner was over, Ella helped with the dishes and was preparing to leave, when Mrs. Ogden called her into the parlor. "I wanted to compliment you on how beautiful you look tonight, and you played very well," she said. "But I didn't know Beethoven put a D-flat chord in that sonata." She winked her eye and Ella smiled.

Mrs. Ogden offered Ella a seat next to hers. "Do you like it at Fisk?" she asked.

"Oh, yes ma'am," Ella answered.

"Would you like to see Fisk modeled after Hampton's manual school program? Please, speak freely," she said.

Ella sat on the edge of her chair. She was happy she'd been asked. She and the other students had been debating the issue among themselves. What was the best educational program for people who had been born slaves? She had an opinion and she was willing to share it.

"As slaves," she began, "we were not allowed to make our own decisions. Everything was decided for us. Now that slavery is over people are still telling us what is best."

Mrs. Ogden listened attentively as Ella continued. "I have no problem with Hampton's program. But I do disagree that it is the best or the only educational program for all black people. It should be our choice. Hampton offers one program. Fisk offers another."

"So you think Fisk should stay as a liberal arts school?"

"Yes, I do."

"So do I," said Mrs. Ogden. "Now we have to convince others to agree with us. Please know that I'm going to work to that end."

Jennie and the other girls were very surprised when Ella told them about her conversation with Mrs. Ogden. They wanted to know what else she said.

"She wants us to perform well at the teacher's conference on Friday. There will be a lot of eyes on us," she explained.

"As long and as hard as we've practiced, we can't help but be good," Jennie said.

When they arrived at the conference, a few members of the association resented the idea that blacks were going to participate.

"You can't do anything about the way some people feel about you," Mr. White said, his eyes flashing with anger. "But you—we—can show the rest of the world how mistaken they are."

Ella remembered the morning she had found the school burned down by the Ku Klux Klan. She had been frightened, but she hadn't been scared off by them.

When the curtains opened for the singers at the convention, a few people booed and hissed. Ella was determined. She knew the Fisk choir sang well. At Mr. White's nod, she walked calmly across the stage, taking her seat at the piano. The audience rewarded her poise and dignity with applause.

Papa would be so proud of me now, she thought. Ella had gone to school and even had private music lessons. But that had ended when her father died of cholera and all his property went to pay unfair lawsuits and creditors who took everything, including her piano. Ella and her stepmother had nothing. That's when the girl had been hired by the American Missionary Association located in Cincinnati to take a teaching job in Gallatin, Tennessee.

Ella played and sang proudly and without fear. To Mr. White's delight, the Teachers' Association gave the Fisk choir a standing ovation. And the choir was asked to come back the next day and the next. What a success!

The good feelings soon gave way to despair when word spread that Fisk might be closing. By 1871, the old barracks building was crumbling and there was no money to buy land for a new site.

"What will happen to us if Fisk closes?" Jennie asked. The answer was too scary to say out loud.

But Ella was hopeful. For the first time she knew something in advance of Jennie. "Do you remember when Mr. White once told us that the cantata was just the beginning? Well, he just gave me a lot of new music to practice. I think he's got a plan to start a touring choir."

And Ella was right. He did.

☆   ☆   ☆

On October 6, 1871, Mr. White, Miss Wells, who went along as the women's chaperone, and eleven Fisk singers set out on a daring venture. Ella felt proud to be with her peers, Maggie L. Porter and Jennie, who sang soprano. Eliza Walker, Phoebe J. Anderson, and Minnie Tate were the altos. Ben Holmes, Thomas Rutling, and George Wells sang tenor, and Greene Evans and Isaac Dickerson sang bass.

Mr. White organized the choir tour to help raise money for the failing school. None of the troupe knew he was using his own money to cover their travel, lodging, and food expenses. It was his hope that after a few concerts, the choir would earn enough money to support itself and any extra would be sent back to Fisk.

But that's not what happened. The tour was a financial disaster. Audiences were large, but contributions were small—so small that by early November the group hardly had money to go on. Kind words, warm wishes, and sincere concern didn't feed thirteen people. Their clothes were ragged. They sang in cold, drafty buildings and lived in private homes that could ill afford to feed them. Still they wouldn't give up.

Things got so bad the soles on Ella's shoes fell off and no amount of patching could hold them together for one more performance. So she made cloth slippers and kept going.

Racial discrimination dogged them every step of the way. Hotels turned them away because of their color. Restaurants refused them service. Sometimes hecklers booed and shouted insults at them. They were literally living from hand to mouth. But none of the singers complained or said they wanted to give up and go home.

One evening Mr. White called for a general meeting. His singers could see he was deeply troubled. "I promised Minnie and Eliza's parents—they being just fourteen—that I'd look after them, see that they didn't get cold or hungry." He swallowed, took a deep breath, then went on. "I've failed. I will not ask you to go on under these conditions."

It was hard for Ella to imagine the mild-mannered New Yorker fighting in the bloody battles at Gettysburg and Chancellorsville, but his eyes had a war-weary glare, a haunted look that suggested all the unspeakable horrors he had endured on the battlefield. His love and concern for them was moving.

"No, no," the singers chimed in.

"We haven't completed our mission," Isaac's big voice boomed.

"But, Isaac, be reasonable. It's wintertime and you don't even have an overcoat." Mr. White turned to the others. "I won't ask you to sing on empty stomachs."

"That's just it," Thomas spoke up. "You're not making us stay. I was made to slave in the fields most of my young life. My suffering and labor benefited no one but my master. But now I've got a chance to do something for myself and my children and their children. Any personal sacrifice is worth that to me. I won't quit."

Ella and the others nodded their agreement. Shy Minnie stood, staying securely close to Jennie and Ella. "My grandmother and mother were freed in Mississippi before the war, and we all moved to a German settlement in Tennessee. My mother gave me five dollars to tuck away, so if something happened, I could come home. You may borrow it," she said, addressing Mr. White.

Softly, Ella began one of the uplifting spirituals.

I ain't got weary yet,
And I ain't got weary yet;
Been down in the valley so long
And I ain't got weary yet.

Before long, the whole group had joined in singing the song they all seemed to know; yet there was no music written for it. When they finished, Mr. White asked, "Ella, what is that song?"

"It's a song of our people," she answered.

"I used to hear my mother sing those songs in the fields and at the church meetings," Ben put in. "And sometimes they were used to send messages about an escape attempt. If a slave was planning a runaway, he'd sing:

Brother, have you come to show me the way?
Brother, have you come to show me the way?
Show me the way how to watch and pray.

or he might sing:

Steal away, Steal away, Steal away home.
I ain't got long to stay here . . . ."

"I've always loved the spirituals of the southern people," said Mr. White, his slender body taking on a happier posture. "I'm sure other people would enjoy knowing about them, too." Ella could tell an idea was forming in Mr. White's head. "Ella, will you select one or two spirituals to add to our program?"

"Does that mean we're going to keep on?" Jennie asked hopefully.

Mr. White looked at the five dollars Minnie had put on the music stand to offer him. "I guess it does."

With the money, Mr. White bought Ben and Isaac winter coats and a pair of shoes for Ella.

After the next concert, Ella wrote a friend at school:

> We added two spirituals to our program and they were greatly received. Our contributions have doubled almost overnight. Mr. White has decided to plan a whole concert based on the spirituals. What a tribute to our fathers and mothers! We are singing their pain and sorrow, their joy and hope . . . .

At last the tide had turned. The spirituals had made the difference. The Fisk Singers were introducing a new sound to the world and transposing the songs of their slave parents into a new art form. The long, dark winter was over. The group returned to Nashville first class.

The Fisk Singers were asked to participate in the World's Peace Jubilee to be held in Boston in June 1873.

More than forty thousand people attended with representatives from all over the world. When it was announced that black singers from Nashville were going to perform "The Battle Hymn of the Republic," a few people booed and jeered.

There were at least twenty thousand people packed in the coliseum. Ella wasn't playing the piano that night. Mr. White had put her in the first soprano position with Jennie as a backup.

A group of black singers from Boston had been asked to sing the first verse, which was set in E-flat, cruelly high-pitched for the average singers. Ella cringed as the other group's soprano slid to the high notes with a quavering voice that bordered on a yowl.

The Fisk Singers were assigned the second verse. Overcoming the indignities they had suffered on the road had made Ella strong. Lifting her voice in clear clean notes she began, "He hath sounded forth the trumpet that shall never call retreat . . . . "

Jennie joined Ella and in one strong voice they sang the next line. Every word rang through the coliseum like a trumpet. When they reached the chorus, the men added their tenor and bass. Twenty thousand people rose to their feet out of respect for the song and the singers.

Glory! Glory! Hallelujah!
Glory! Glory! Hallelujah!
Glory! Glory! Hallelujah!
His truth is marching on!

Ella reached out and took Jennie's hand. Tears streamed from their eyes. When they reached the high E at the climax of the hymn, the voices of those thirteen young people were second to none. And the crowd knew it.

Ladies waved their handkerchiefs. Men hurled their hats in the air and shouted cheers, "The Jubilees! The Jubilees! The Jubilees forever!"

And the Fisk Jubilee Singers were born.

Ella Sheppard never forgot that night, although there were many more proud moments in their history. She and Jennie remained with the Singers when they went to Europe. On the passenger ship going over, they performed at the captain's request. They sang a medley of spirituals and ended with:

Wade in the water,
Wade in the water, children.
Wade in the water.
God's gonna trouble de water.

In Europe they were received by large and enthusiastic crowds. The English people loved their music. Word spread that a group of young black students were singing their way across Europe, winning hearts and raising money to support their own dreams. Everything the singers earned, they sent back to their school. They raised the money to build Jubilee Hall, the first building at the present-day site of Fisk University in Nashville. Fisk became known the world over for its fine liberal arts education, outstanding faculty, and proud alumni.

Today, a new generation of Jubilee Singers continues to entertain and to teach the world about the spirituals of the African American people.

COUNTRY BOY TO CONGRESSMAN

THE STORY OF CORDELL HULL

Cordell Hull was a world-class diplomat, honored around the globe. When he left Tennessee at the age of thirty-six to go to Washington, D.C., he was a freshman congressman from the Fourth Tennessee District. His biographical sketch in the *Congressional Directory* stated:

> *Cordell Hull, Democrat, of Carthage, was born October 2, 1871, in Overton (now Pickett) County, Tennessee; was graduated from the Law Department of Cumberland University, Lebanon, Tennessee, and was a lawyer by profession; was a member of the lower house of the state legislature two terms; served in the Fourth Regiment, Tennessee Volunteer Infantry, during the Spanish-American War, with the rank of captain. Later was appointed by the governor, and afterward elected judge of the fifth judicial district, which position was resigned during his race for Congress . . . .*

These accomplishments were outstanding, but they are by no means a complete record. He would go on to serve as secretary of state under President Franklin D. Roosevelt (1933–44). He would also found the United Nations and win a Nobel Peace Prize. But he always recognized his roots and often said with pride, "I am a citizen of the state of Tennessee."

His pride in his state has since been returned in full. Today, Cordell Hull stands high in the ranks among the men and women who have contributed to the cause of world peace. This is his story.

"Come go fishin' with us, Cord," Wyoming shouted as he rounded the house with his pole and minnow bucket.

Cordell looked up from his book. "Too busy," he answered his brother quickly.

"Come on, Cord. It's Saturday. No need to study on Saturday," his little brother Roy pleaded.

The screen door creaked open. Their father stepped out on the long front porch. "That's how come Cord's gonna get ahead in this world," William Hull said gruffly. "He studies when he don't have to. Now you boys run along to fishin', and leave your brother be."

The younger boys shrugged. Then they hurried across the field and down to the creek. Their shouts of joy echoed back to the porch where Cordell held a book with the same enthusiasm his brothers showed as they baited a hook.

There wasn't a whole lot he could do about his love of learning. It all seemed to come naturally. He was glad that

Wyoming and Roy understood and held no hard feelings about his turning them down. In the same way, they had come to accept the favoritism their father showed him. There wasn't much Cordell could do about that either.

William Hull was fondly called "Uncle Billy" by everybody around Willow Grove and Byrdstown, including his five sons. And everybody, including the other four boys, knew Cordell was Uncle Billy's favorite child. In many families that might have caused conflict, but everybody who knew Cordell understood he was special, a model for others to follow. Cordell was sandwiched between two older and two younger brothers. He was tall like his older brothers and every bit as tough. He had a no-nonsense way of handling himself.

Cordell shaded his eyes with his hands and watched his younger brothers disappear into the woods. Then he turned to his father who was still standing on the porch.

"Is Ma feeling better?" he asked.

" 'Bout the same. Her legs are paining her pretty bad. It's the fall time of the year," Uncle Billy said, sniffing the air. "Weather's changing—first hot, then cold. It makes her rheumatism act up mighty fierce."

"Do you think she'll be able to come to the school debate next week?"

"Don't know. She wants to come. But not to worry! I'll be there to hear you talk circles 'round them other whippersnappers." Uncle Billy slapped his thigh and laughed heartily.

Cordell laughed, too. But winning the debate against his classmates wasn't going to be as simple as his father made it sound. The parents in the Willow Grove community had started the debating society at the school. Everybody took the debates seriously and followed the arguments closely. The debaters all wanted to do well, but none more than Cordell, who'd been reading about his subject every spare minute.

Uncle Billy always expected a lot from Cordell, and he obliged his father as best he could. After all, Uncle Billy was a man to be admired. He was a shrewd businessman and a hard worker. He had made a little money working his one-hundred-acre farm after the Civil War. And despite the fact that he, like so many of his neighbors, didn't have much education, he had managed to open his own store and post office and to hire a teacher for his boys and the neighborhood children.

Now it was time for the boys to go on to higher education. Orestes and Senadius, Cordell's older brothers, were going to a school in Willow Bend. But they, unlike Cordell, weren't too excited about education.

The Hulls, like most backwoods families of the 1880s, couldn't afford to send all their children all the way through school. Cordell and his brothers knew that Uncle Billy would use the debate to decide which of them showed the most promise and which would go on in school.

On the night of the debate, Cordell found his father's square-chinned face in the crowd. Ma hadn't been able to walk, but she'd fortified Cordell with love and many well-wishes. He touched the linen handkerchief in his pocket that she had given him earlier that evening. It had belonged to his great-grandfather, Allen B. Hull, who'd come to Tennessee before it was a state. Many times, Cordell had gone with his parents to the Nash Cemetery near Armathwaite where his grandparents were buried. "Grandpa Hull's hankie will give you luck," his mama had whispered.

Three speakers had gone before him, and the third one was concluding. Cordell was next. He feared that when his name was called, he might stand there speechless as he'd done several years ago. He heard his name called and stood up.

"Who deserves more recognition?" Cordell began, gaining confidence as he went. "Explorer Christopher Columbus or General George Washington? They are both important in the development of American history. Without Christopher Columbus's discovery there would have been no need for George Washington. But without George Washington there would be no United States . . . . "

He skillfully presented both sides of the argument, defending Columbus over Washington and then shifting to praise Washington over Columbus. Cordell didn't try to convince his audience that one man's contribution was more important than the other. "Our nation is not great because of the independent actions of one or two men," he said convincingly. "Our nation became great because of the courage, hard work, and dedication of many people like Washington and Columbus."

When he sat down, the crowd burst into thunderous applause. They were surprised and pleased with his presentation. Uncle Billy was beside himself with pride.

"You've got a good talker there," his friends and neighbors said, giving Cordell an honor reserved for men four times his age.

Uncle Billy decided that night that Cordell would be the son he'd send to school—as far as he wanted to go.

Cordell always knew he wanted to be a lawyer, and he never changed his mind. At sixteen Cordell was well over six feet tall, strong and healthy. He made excellent grades at Montvalle School over in Celina, the county seat of Clay County. Joe S. McMillin was the principal and teacher who influenced him as much as Uncle Billy. Through McMillin's recommendation, Cordell and his older brother Orestes went to National Normal University in Lebanon, Ohio. Then in 1891, Cordell graduated from law school at Cumberland University in Lebanon, Tennessee.

Soon Cordell opened a law office in Celina. He was only twenty, but success had made him confident in his ability.

"I'm going to run for the state legislature," Cordell told Joe McMillin.

"But you're not old enough to hold office," Joe protested. "You've got to be twenty-one. Why, you can't even vote for yourself."

Cordell had thought it through carefully. "I'm twenty now, but by the time I take office, I'll be twenty-one."

"If you win!"

"Oh," he said, blushing slightly. "If I win . . . of course." But losing wasn't part of his plan.

"Sure, I'll support you," Joe answered, "but my brother Benton could do you the most good."

Cordell knew this was true. He had gotten to know Benton during law school when Joe had arranged for Cordell to drive his brother to political meetings. Joe had also helped Cordell get a job with his other brother John McMillin, a well-known lawyer in Nashville and Celina, before and during law school.

Cordell was grateful to Joe and his family, but right now Joe was not being very encouraging.

"Your opponent is a more experienced campaigner than you are," he warned him. But Cordell would not back down. "Besides," Joe continued, "you're a bit too polished for your own good." Joe was referring to Cordell's handsome face, neat appearance, and well-mannered attitude.

Cordell understood why Joe thought he needed to put more flair in his campaign speeches. "You've got natural flare," the younger man objected. "I don't and I know it. Now, if I show myself to be more or less than what I am, that wouldn't be honest."

Cordell went ahead with his campaign using his own style. He was not, as Joe complained, an exciting speaker like some other politicians. But his sincerity won the trust of the voters.

So, on the first Monday in January 1893, Cordell took the oath of office as state representative from Carthage to the Tennessee legislature. He remembered Joe's advice as he made his first move into politics. It was a moment he would relive many times as he filled offices in the years to come.

Cordell Hull returned from serving in the Spanish-American War in 1899. This firsthand view of bloody fighting left him determined to seek peaceful ways to end conflicts. Talking things through with people who differed with him had worked on a personal level. Why couldn't it work for countries?

These and other thoughts were on the veteran's mind when he returned to the hills of Tennessee. And thoughts of promoting peace, thoughts which would stay with him all his life, also influenced his actions while he was a circuit judge in the Fifth Judicial District.

As a circuit judge, Cordell had to travel from his new home in Gainesboro to the county seats of all ten counties in his district. Legal cases had to wait to be decided until he arrived. It was a tough schedule!

While listening to cases in Gainesboro, Jamestown, Carthage, Cookeville, Crossville, and other towns, Cordell gained quite a reputation for being tough but fair. People would come from miles around to listen to him give decisions.

"Good to meet you, Judge," a new secretary greeted Cordell at the Jamestown courthouse. "Will you be starting court at eight or nine in the morning?"

"The docket looks lighter than usual, but I'll still hold to eight." Judge Hull knew that the lawyers on his circuit had been complaining about his early starts, but he held firmly to his time.

"Order in the court," he said, hammering his gavel. The public seats were quickly filled, and the cases passed one after the other until lunch. He'd heard criminal cases all morning. He would hear civil cases in the afternoon.

"Sir, there's a man asking to see you over at the Mark Twain Hotel," the secretary said after the session was over.

"Did he say who he was?" Judge Hull asked hanging up his robes.

"No, sir. But he's all in a fit to see you. Says he knows you well."

"Do you doubt the man's word?"

"No, sir. But he's dressed rather shabbily in overalls. And he was carrying the most peculiar paper suitcase."

By that time, Cordell was chuckling. "Is the man about my height? White hair that's parted down the middle?"

The clerk nodded yes to both questions.

"And is the man clutching the suitcase as though it contained at least $5,000?"

"Do you know this man, Judge? Or maybe I should ask," he added showing some embarrassment, "should I know this man?"

"You're new here in Jamestown. I wouldn't expect you to know him. No doubt you've heard about him though. That's my father."

"Bill Hull? Is that really Uncle Billy?"

Cordell was not surprised at the man's reaction. Uncle Billy often came to see him at work, and by now he had become something of a celebrity in the eyes of the local citizens. Like most old-timers, Uncle Billy always had at least three good stories to tell about the Civil War.

Cordell left the courthouse in Jamestown and walked across the square to the hotel, the site the house of the father of Samuel

Clemens (Mark Twain). Cordell found his father in the dining room, and the two men sat down to have dinner together.

"You were mighty tough on those two lawyers, I hear," Uncle Billy said.

Cordell sighed. How many times had he told his father not to discuss cases outside the courtroom? It didn't matter.

"People stretch the truth sometimes," Cordell answered with a grin.

But Uncle Billy had heard the truth. Two lawyers had refused to heed Judge Hull's repeated warnings to stop arguing with each other and present their cases to the court. When he realized both lawyers had been drinking, he ordered them handcuffed together until they sobered up.

"Serves those two right." Uncle Billy sided with Cordell.

"I know folk say I'm tough, especially about public drunkenness. Some of these guys think they can shoot up the town and endanger people's lives and get off by saying it was all in fun. Well, not with me!"

Uncle Billy held a spoon on his finger. "Balance," he said. "Justice and mercy—make sure they're balanced, son."

"Excuse me, " a woman approached them in the dining room. Uncle Billy recognized her. "Julia Hamby! How long has it been?"

"Years now," she said.

"Cordell, this here is Julia Hamby. It was her family, the Lovelesses, who found me dying on the side of the road. I'd been left for dead by thieves, and I would have been too, if not for them nursing me back to health. I'm ever beholden."

The woman was clearly upset. "Judge Hull, " she said in a pleading voice, "my son is not bad. John hardly ever drinks. But he's gone and got himself in trouble. I'm a lone widow, and he's my sole support. If he's fined, we got the money to pay it, but then we won't have money to pay on our farm. And I don't know how we'll get through the coming winter."

The judge promised to listen to the evidence and base his decision on that. On the next day, Cordell fined John Hamby fifty dollars. There was a gasp in the courtroom. Cordell saw Uncle Billy's face turn dark with concern.

"But sir, that's excessively high," one of the lawyers argued.

"The court has ruled," Cordell answered cutting the lawyer off curtly.

That evening, Cordell drove out to the widow's farm. Her red-rimmed eyes flashed anger and surprise when she saw the judge at her door.

"Well?" she said, eyeing him suspiciously.

"May I come in?"

"What do you want?" she asked in a stiff tone.

"This morning I was a judge. I did my duty," he said. "Now I've come just as a concerned friend." He placed an envelope on the table and left quickly.

Inside the envelope was fifty dollars.

Cordell stood before the U. S. House of Representatives early in 1916 to speak about the threat of war: "Strange as it may seem, one peaceable and peace-loving country after another has been drawn [into the war], under circumstances impossible to avoid without such sacrifices of honor and of God-given rights as no country could make and long endure."

Since his election in 1907, Cordell had become known as the "bit-too-serious-Tennessean." But he quickly earned respect for many of his ideas, especially those about foreign policy.

His wisdom was now being called on as never before while World War I raged in Europe. Cordell had watched in frustration as the fighting began. And now that Germany had launched a massive attack on Verdun, the Allies (Great Britain, France, Italy, and Russia) needed help from the United States more than ever.

"I'm so tired of watching our young men die, Rose," Cordell sighed. He had recently married Rose Whitney from Virginia. She squeezed his hand sympathetically. She knew that the proud Tennessean would make any sacrifice to establish a lasting peace.

Even after the American army, under the leadership of General John ("Black Jack") Pershing, had helped secure a victory for the Allies, Congressman Hull continued to worry about the future.

President Woodrow Wilson responded to the end of the war by putting forth the Fourteen Points, a peace plan that led to the formation of the League of Nations. Democracy seemed safe, but Cordell could not help wondering how long the peace would last.

He had other reasons to worry as well. In 1920 he suffered his first and last political defeat. To the surprise of many, he lost his seat in Congress to Wynne ("Windy") Clouse. Some thought that his career was hurt when President Wilson lost his bid for reelection, but Cordell had other ideas.

"What hurt you?" a reporter asked him.

Cordell replied with the single word: "Women."

"What?" the reporter asked in surprise. "Are you saying that because women got the right to vote, they cost you the election?"

"Just the opposite. Women got the vote, but they didn't vote! That's what hurt me."

After that, Cordell worked hard at getting more women out to vote. But other problems could not be so easily addressed. Three years after this defeat, Uncle Billy died. Cordell was left to go on with his life and his dreams of world peace, without the support of his father who had first inspired him.

But with Rose at his side, Cordell pushed on. His political career and his trips to Washington were far from over. By the time he returned to Congress, this time as a senator from Tennessee, he had already served as the chairman of the Democratic National Committee. Then, in 1933, President Franklin Roosevelt asked him to serve as the secretary of state.

As the years passed, Cordell knew that the world was on the brink of another war. In 1940, he supported President Roosevelt for a third term because he felt it would be a mistake to "change horses in the middle of a stream." But who was to be the number-two man on the ticket? The President was holding his cards very close to his chest.

One night, the telephone at the Hulls rang. Secretary Hull answered it. President Roosevelt's quick voice leaped right to the point.

"I want you to be my running mate. What do you say about that? We'd be hard to beat!"

"Mr. President, I'm honored," Cordell answered with feeling. He admired President Roosevelt almost as much as he had Uncle Billy. They were always very formal with each other, even though they had, by this time, known each other for years.

"Is that a yes, Mr. Secretary?"

There was a moment of silence. "No, sir. I'm honored, but I can't acccept. My age and health . . . "

"Let's not bring up age and health. Our opponents are going to talk about that enough," Roosevelt joked.

"My answer is still no, sir," he answered. Saying no to his President was like saying no to his country, and Cordell found it hard to do. But he was convinced he should not run for office.

Not willing to take no for an answer, the President said, "Let me speak to Mrs. Hull. Maybe I can convince her."

"I'm sorry, sir, but Mrs. hull has already retired for the evening."

There were a few more exchanges, and the conversation ended.

Rose Hull put down her knitting. "Did you just turn down the vice presidency?" she asked.

"No, I turned down the presidency. If anything should happen to President Roosevelt, I don't want to be president."

Even without Cordell as running mate, Roosevelt was reelected in 1940. As early as 1935 Secretary Hull had predicted the coming of the war in Europe, writing to the *New York Times:* "Europe is headed for a terrific smashup unless some new influence . . . comes into the picture . . . The United States and other American countries will suffer intensely, even if not directly involved."

Cordell, much to his dismay, was right. Germany invaded Poland in 1939, and in 1941 Pearl Harbor was attacked by the Japanese. The world was at war again, and the United States was once again allied with England and Russia.

"When will it all end, Rose? When will the wars stop?" Cordell would often ask his wife. "There simply has to be a way to make it harder to start a war—to get nations to talk to one another."

As if in answer to his own question, Secretary Hull began planning a postwar peace organization in the center of a raging war. With President Roosevelt's help, he would find a way.

"It is *not* too soon to start thinking about after the war," Cordell protested to the President. "I'd like to organize a committee to explore possibilities. I want to involve both Democrats and Republicans, because we need both parties' support if we are to create an international organization in which the United States will be a member along with other nations."

The President approved Secretary Hull's proposal, but added, "I don't know how you'll pull it off."

Cordell stopped at the door of the Oval Office. "Mr. President," he said over his shoulder. "I had two older brothers and two younger brothers. I learned how to negotiate a long time ago!"

It took a lot of careful negotiation to get the committee to think of the organization as neither Republican nor Democratic. But Secretary Hull managed to do it. It took just as much effort to get the idea of a world peace organization taken seriously when most of the countries in the world were fighting each other. But Secretary Hull struggled to keep the idea alive, and President and Mrs. Roosevelt supported him.

In spite of his failing health, President Roosevelt was nominated by the Democratic Party to run for a fourth term in 1944. It was during the election that President Roosevelt made the plans for a United Nations organization public.

Secretary Hull was standing beside him as he said, "The maintenance of peace and security must be the joint task of all peace-loving nations. We have, therefore, sought to develop plans for an international organization comprising all such nations . . . . "

Then on October 2, 1944, one month before the election, Cordell got sick and had to leave the State Department. For days he drifted in and out of consciousness, tossing and turning in his sleep. He thought he saw Uncle Billy. They were hunting for something . . . no, someone. Uncle Billy was hunting down the men who had robbed him and left him to die on the road. *No! No!* Cordell cried out in his mind. *Violence is not the answer.* But Uncle Billy didn't hear him. He fired the gun anyway.

Cordell heard his brother's voice, reminding him of the term they'd spent at National Normal School in Ohio. It was the first time he'd ever been on a train. "I caught the flu and had to go home to the hills to recover," he mumbled, "before the term was over."

"What a waste," all his father's friends had said. "What a shame he had to get sick and lose a whole term in school."

Cordell awoke to find Rose sitting beside his bed with a worried look on her face. His mouth was hot and dry.

"Was it a waste?" he asked.

Rose jumped up and came to the bedside. "You've been very ill," she said with tears in her eyes. "But I think the crisis has passed. You'll be fine."

"Nothing you do is ever a waste," he said, answering his own question. "I got sick and had to go home, but I got a broader vision—experiences that were different. So it was not a waste. Not then, or now."

"No, dear, your work has never been a waste."

"Don't resign," Roosevelt said. "Stay on until after the election."

"That wouldn't be fair to the country. I must resign."

"But what about all the work you've done? We're going to win this war, and the world's going to need this organization you've worked so hard to develop. You can't quit now."

"The work I've done will not end. I must resign," he said. And so he did on November 30, 1944.

Several months after being reelected, President Roosevelt died, but not before he had helped to insure Cordell's dream. Cordell Hull was appointed as a member of the American delegation to the San Francisco Conference. Representatives from all around the world came to the United States to form the United Nations.

Cordell was the senior adviser, but he was still too ill to travel. He and Secretary of State Edward R. Stettinius talked every day.

One day in early June 1945, Cordell had just finished having lunch with Rose when a messenger came with the news that the founding nations had approved a charter. "The United Nations" was the organization's official name.

It was a proud day when he signed the charter. Someone whisked away the pen he used to keep as a souvenir.

"Just before leaving for the Spanish-American war," he told a friend later, "my regiment gathered in the town square, back in Carthage, Tennessee, to say good-bye to our family and friends. I happened to have on a tie," he said remembering, "that had stars on it. The folk took the tie off and cut it into pieces and passed them out so as never to forget the war. I hope the pen will be remembered for its part in peace."

Cordell's wish came true. He could never forget any of the three wars he had seen, and his dedication to the dream of promoting world peace will never be forgotten by the people of Tennessee.

As he stood to accept the Nobel Peace Prize, the seventy-four-year-old man graciously spoke to his nation and the world:

> For many years I have devoted my life to the study and preparation of an international organization that would promote harmonious interaction among the countries of the world. The task is done. Now I leave it in others' hands, but I am confident that with reasonable understanding among the nations the organization can move forward.

The last ten years of Cordell Hull's life gave him a chance to watch his prediction come true. The United Nations did indeed move forward. In 1955 Cordell Hull died at the age of eighty-four, knowing that his dreams had been fulfilled.

OTHER BOOKS TO READ

THOMAS SHARPE SPENCER

Bond, Octavia Zollicoffer. *Old Tales Retold: Or Perils and Adventures of Tennessee Pioneers.* Nashville: Smith & Lamar, Publishing House of the Methodist Episcopal Church, 1914.

Elliott, Lizzie P. *Early History of Nashville.* Nashville: The Board of Education, 1911.

Ganier, Albert F. *The Wildlife Met by Tennessee's First Settlers.* Nashville: The Tennessee Ornithological Society, 1915.

Parks, Edd Winfield. *Long Hunter: The Story of Big-Foot Spencer.* New York: Farrar & Rinehart, 1942.

Shelton, Ferne, ed. and Helen K. More, comp. *Pioneer Superstitions: Old-Timey Signs and Sayings.* High Point: Hutcraft Publishing Company, 1969.

NANCY WARD

Alderman, Pat. *Nancy Ward, Cherokee Chieftainess: Her Cry Was All for Peace. Dragging Canoe, Cherokee-Chickamauga War Chief: We are Not Yet Conquered,* 2d ed. Johnson City: The Overmountain Press, 1990.

Alderman, Pat. *The Overmountain Men.* Johnson City: The Overmountain Press, 1970.

Bond, Octavia Zollicoffer. *Old Tales Retold: Or Perils and Adventures of Tennessee Pioneers.* Nashville: Smith & Lamar, Publishing House of the Methodist Episcopal. Church, 1914.

ELLA SHEPPARD AND THE FISK JUBILEE SINGERS

Marsh, J.B.T. *The Story of the Jubilee Singers with Their Songs. Rev. ed.* New York: Negro University Press, 1903.

Merriam, Lucius Salisbury, Ph.D. *Higher Education in Tennessee.* Washington: Government Printing Office, 1893.

Pike, G.D. *The Jubilee Singers, Campaign for Twenty Thousand Dollars.* New York: Lee & Shepard Publishers, 1873.

Tipton, C. Robert. *The Fisk Jubilee Singers.* Missionary Herald, 1947.

CORDELL HULL

Hull, Cordell. *The Memoirs of Cordell Hull, 2 vols.* New York: MacMillan, 1948.

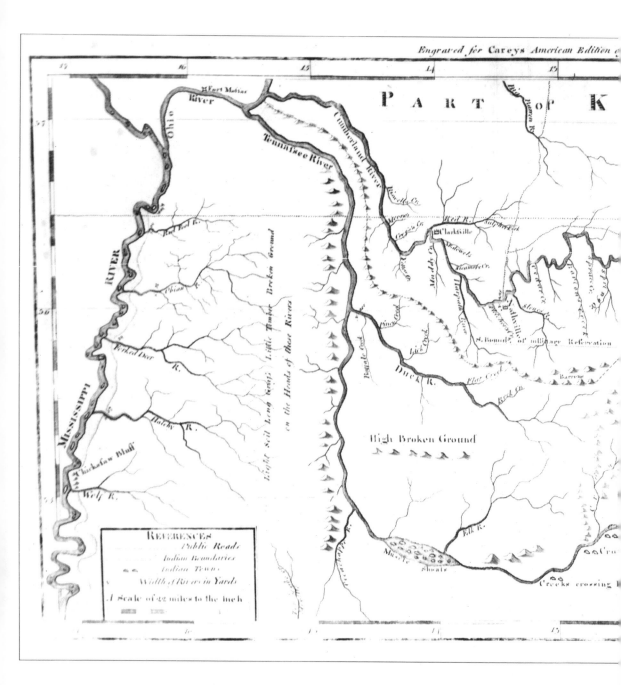